Stephen Salisbury, Levi Lincoln

Proceedings of the American Antiquarian Society, at the

semi-annual meeting, held in Boston, April 26, 1865

Stephen Salisbury, Levi Lincoln

Proceedings of the American Antiquarian Society, at the semi-annual meeting, held in Boston, April 26, 1865

ISBN/EAN: 9783337713447

Printed in Europe, USA, Canada, Australia, Japan

Cover: Foto ©ninafisch / pixelio.de

More available books at **www.hansebooks.com**

PROCEEDINGS

OF THE

AMERICAN ANTIQUARIAN SOCIETY,

AT THE

SEMI-ANNUAL MEETING, HELD IN BOSTON,

April 26, 1865.

BOSTON:

PRESS OF JOHN WILSON AND SON,

No. 15, Water Street.

1865.

PROCEEDINGS.

Hon. STEPHEN SALISBURY, President, in the chair.

The Secretary, Hon. EDWARD MELLEN, being absent, detained by professional business, STEPHEN SALISBURY, Jr., was chosen Secretary *pro tempore.*

The Record of the last meeting was read.

The Report of the Council, prepared by JOSEPH SARGENT, M.D., was then read. The Reports of the Treasurer and of the Librarian having been adopted as a part of this Report, the Treasurer, NATHANIEL PAINE, Esq., read his Report; and SAMUEL F. HAVEN, Esq., the Librarian, read his Report.

The Report was discussed, with much interest and commendation, by Hon. Emory Washburn, Rev. Dr. George E. Ellis, J. Wingate Thornton, Esq., and Hon. Ira M. Barton; and, on motion of Hon. ROBERT C. WINTHROP, the Report was accepted, and referred to the Publishing Committee for publication.

Hon. LEVI LINCOLN, with a few heartfelt and impressive words, offered the following Resolutions, for

record, as the sentiments of the Society, in regard to
the death of the President of the United States: —

Resolved, That, in the death of Abraham Lincoln, the honored
and beloved Chief Magistrate of this nation, by the hand of a mis-
creant assassin, a deplorable calamity has been brought upon the
Government and people of the United States, and personal grief to
the heart of every loyal citizen in the land.

Resolved, That, in the election of Abraham Lincoln to the
office of President of the United States, and in his administration
of the Government, during a most threatening and perilous cri-
sis of affairs, the country has found protection and safe guidance;
the people have been saved from anarchy, and the nation from
disunion. Through his wisdom and patriotism and constancy and
moral heroism, *traitors* have been awed, and Rebellion repressed;
our armies have triumphed; and peace, as we trust, is about to
be restored to a bleeding and suffering land.

Resolved, That the character of our late Chief Magistrate was
distinguished by all the attributes of a great and good man. As
a statesman, he comprehended the vast interests, and discerned
the threatening dangers, of the nation; while his policy and his
measures gave efficiency to the mandates of authority, and inspired
patriotism, courage, and confidence in the people. His love of
liberty was as intense as his devotion of service to country; and
he labored to secure to the humblest citizen the rights enjoyed by
the most favored. His life was made illustrious by exemplary
purity and the manly virtues, and furnishes an instructive example, to all future time, of the inappreciable glory of private worth
crowned with public honors.

Resolved, That, in the terrible strife of civil warfare through
which the nation is now passing, the wisdom of his counsels, the
firmness of his resolves, the calm consistency and unfaltering
energy of his action, all conspiring to the maintenance of consti-
tutional government, and the preservation of the integrity of the
nation, and blessed, of the good providence of God, to that end,
will inscribe, in letters of light, on the record of history, the name
of Abraham Lincoln, as the CONSERVATOR OF THE REPUBLIC!

These resolutions were seconded by members; and President SALISBURY then addressed the Society as follows : —

GENTLEMEN, — The incumbent duty of this Society, as patriots and devoted servants in one of the temples of history, to hold up to admiration and imitation the wisdom and virtues of a Chief Magistrate, whose beneficent life has been terminated by assassination, will be well performed. Your memorial of honor will be erected by your associate, who is no stranger to the high qualities of statesmanship and official fidelity, which he has so worthily praised. I will not attempt to add to the effect of this participation in the emotions which occupy the mind of every American patriot. But I invite you to turn your thoughts, for the briefest moment, to the great lesson of the day, — the demonstration of the vitality and strength of democratic institutions. Foreign nations, and men of future ages, will contemplate with approbation and sympathy the expression of affectionate grief, which rose through the length and breadth of the continent, for the loss of the personal character and administrative ability of Abraham Lincoln. But, in the distant view of space and time, the political condition of our country, under this fatal attack on the representative of its sovereignty, will be the conspicuous object of the greatest interest and admiration and profound astonishment. With subtle cunning, it was contrived to remove at once the two lives which seemed most necessary to the existence of the Government. For a moment, the twofold crime seemed to be successful; but the expected effect utterly failed. There was no opportunity for a *coup d'état*, nor for the slightest disturbance of the operations of the Government. The mighty framework of popular sovereignty was not broken, was not shaken, by an incident which would probably have scattered in fragments a monarchy of Europe. In the first years of our struggle for national life, fearful predictions were fulminated against our country by the possessors and supporters of arbitrary power, until the gathering forces of democratic progress in Europe, which were so numerous in the view of De Tocqueville, seemed to have dwindled down to a few sturdy individuals. We were told that our desired enlargement of the area of freedom would result in the abrogation of all natural human rights, which Government would be bound to respect. We were admonished that the farce of self-government had been played out, and our national defence was impossible, because loyalty so necessarily depended on the personal permanence of political power, that it could not exist in the mutations of an elective Government; and many of our own citizens sorrowfully assented to this opinion, until it was gloriously refuted by the generous self-devotion and the unexampled fraternal feeling of the whole people. We were also reminded, in most degrading terms, of our characteristic desire for pecuniary independence, and the means of happy and improving life, as a proof of the basest selfishness ; and we were taunted with the dependence of our national wealth on the great staple, which we must seek from the rebels. All these discouragements, and the labor and cost of the contest, never for a moment disposed the people to quail or falter, or shrink from any call of their chosen rulers for service or sacrifice. In all this night of suffering and trial, this nation has been led by the hand that guides the stars, in a way it knew not, to objects which it would not have attempted to reach. And, when the harbor of enduring peace and prosperity seemed to be in near prospect, the beloved pilot, who only was deemed to be competent to his Herculean task, was slain at the helm. While we weep, we will thank God, that not a spar nor a plank has been displaced, and our course is steady and unchanged. Our own poet must have seen in vision this day, when he said, —

> " Sail on, sail on, O Ship of State !
> Sail on, O Union, strong and great !
> Humanity, with all its fears,
> With all the hopes of future years,
> Is hanging breathless on thy fate ;
> In spite of rock and tempest's roar,
> In spite of false lights on the shore,
> Sail on, nor fear to breast the sea :
> Our hearts, our hopes, are all with thee ! "

The resolutions were unanimously adopted by a standing vote.

Rev. JONAS KING, D.D., of Athens, Greece, and

Rev. CALVIN E. STOWE, D.D., of Hartford, Conn., recommended by the Council, were elected members by ballot.

SAMUEL F. HAVEN, Esq., in behalf of the Committee of Publication, verbally reported, that that Committee had not been inattentive to their duties; but the limited amount of the Publishing Fund, and the high cost of printing, obliged them to publish less frequently than the abundance of interesting subjects possessed by the Society rendered desirable. It is proposed that the next volume of transactions shall be a reprint of Thomas's " History of Printing," with extensive and valuable additions committed to the Society by Dr. THOMAS, and with other important additions. Dr. N. B. SHURTLEFF expressed a high opinion of the value, and the public demand for, such a publication. This Report was accepted.

Hon. I. M. BARTON, for the Committee on a Publication of the Catalogue of Members of the Society, reported progress; and, on his suggestion, it was voted, that the same Committee be requested to continue their work, and to report to the Society on the expediency of a change of the By-laws, to enlarge the number of American members; and the meeting was dissolved.

STEPHEN SALISBURY, JR.
Recording Secretary pro tempore.

REPORT OF THE COUNCIL.

The American Antiquarian Society, meeting in this period of our nation's sorrow, cannot be unmindful of the occasion. The solemnity of grief is still around us. The darkness is greater for following so suddenly upon such a blaze of light. The silence of a great people under affliction, their magnanimous forbearance, their earnest confidence and trust, are a sublime spectacle, such as the world has never before seen. In our struggle for national life, they are the panoply of spiritual armor with which God girds us for the right.

As the Rebellion was an assault upon democratic institutions, a violent declaration that the majority should not rule, so was the assassination of the President a blow upon the Republic. The recoil will astonish the nations. Democratic institutions will survive; and already a stronger life, purified by the breath of the Almighty, throbs through the heart of the great Republic.

It is not for us, nor is it yet the time, to write the Eulogy of Abraham Lincoln. His own language, now sad and sublime, is his best memorial. "With

2

malice towards no one, with charity for all, with firmness in the right, as God gives us to see the right, let
us strive on to finish the work we are in; to bind up
the nation's wound; to care for him who shall have
borne the battle, and for his widow and his orphans;
to do all which may achieve and cherish a just and
lasting peace among ourselves, and with all nations."
With what more fit words on his lips could the Christian statesman enter the portals of heaven!

Since our last regular meeting, the Society has lost,
in the death of the Hon. Edward Everett, one of its
most distinguished associates. For several years our
President, his learning and his example have been
our honor and our ornament. Erudite in all language, he was not a mere linguist, but read history
and philosophy in the structure of language, and
was an antiquary from the earliest. Of complete
and symmetrical education, his life was elegant, clas-
sic, and conservative. Of universal learning, he was
equal in all he undertook, and "adorned all that
he touched." Himself an important element in our
national history for the last quarter of a century, he
stepped forward in his country's trial, forgetful of
conservatism and of prejudice and of association, to
offer the fulness of his wisdom, of his statesmanship,
and of his peculiar power. Of few can it be so well
said, that his life was his eulogy.

At a special meeting of the Society, called to commemorate this sad event, addresses were made by several members; whose publication, with the transactions of the Society, renders any more extended notice by the Council unnecessary.

On the 20th of October last, died, at Copenhagen, Carl Christian Rafn, the distinguished Danish antiquary, who had been a member of this Society for nearly thirty years. He was born at Braesborg, in the Island of Funen, in Denmark, on the 16th of January, 1795. At a very early age, he devoted himself to the study of the Icelandic tongue, which, in ancient times, had been the universal language of the north of Europe, and became distinguished for his knowledge of the Sagas, and other forms of early Scandinavian literature. He was the founder of the Royal Society of Northern Antiquaries, and the editor of its principal publications. He is best known in this country by the large work entitled " Antiquitates Americanæ, sive Scriptores Septentrionales Rerum Ante-Columbiarum, in America," comprising the records contained in the old sagas, the annals and geographical works of the North, on the voyages of discovery undertaken by the Scandinavians to America, in the tenth, eleventh, twelfth, thirteenth, and fourteenth centuries. These venerable and obscure manuscripts are translated and annotated by him, and illustrated by numerous maps and drawings. If his interpretation of relics and monuments in this country has not always been accepted as reliable, the great value and general truth of his historical developments are not denied. His memoir on the discovery of America has been translated into most languages, and has received the approbation of the learned of all civilized nations. Since the publication of that work, the exploits of the Northmen in the Eastern countries have engaged his attention; and he has developed, from the same sources, the part which the Scandinavians have played, at remote periods, in Russia, and at Constantinople under the Roman emperors.

His literary labors were otherwise varied and numerous. The world has lost in him a man of extensive and peculiar learning; and his own country, a most useful and distinguished citizen.

Professor Benjamin Silliman, who died on the 24th of November last, was one of the oldest and earliest members of this Society, having been elected in September, 1813. It is well known that he was chiefly devoted to natural science; but in that scientific publication which he established, and long sustained by his personal labors, were inserted, from time to time, many valuable contributions to the archæology of this country, — a subject in which he formerly took much interest. In his own special departments of study, Professor Silliman always held a most prominent position. He entered upon his duties, as Professor of Chemistry and Natural History at Yale College, in

1804, and continued to teach or lecture till 1853. Besides editing the " American Journal of Science and Arts," he wrote and edited a number of scientific text-books and treatises, and gave lectures on his favorite topics in most of our principal cities.

His " Journal of Travels in England, Holland, and Scotland," published in 1810, was a very successful literary production, and has been popular with all classes of readers. Few men have been more loved and respected, and few have so happily completed a long and well-rounded life of usefulness and honor. He was born August 8, 1779, and was therefore more than eighty-five years old at the time of his death.

Henry R. Schoolcraft, who died Dec. 10, 1864, aged seventy-one, has long been widely celebrated for his works on Indian history, and his knowledge of their languages and customs. His last and largest labor in that field of study was in compiling and editing the six solid quarto volumes, published under the direction of the United-States Commissioner of Indian Affairs, entitled " History, Condition, and Prospects of the Indian Tribes of the United States." This work, made attractive, as well as instructive, by profuse illustration, will be an honorable and durable monument to Mr. Schoolcraft's memory.

William B. Fowle, who died at Medfield, Feb. 7, 1865, at the age of sixty-nine, was a nephew and executor of Rev. Dr. Bentley, of Salem, one of the benefactors of this Society. He has not taken an active interest in our Institution, except in carrying out the provisions of his uncle's will. He was a teacher for some years, and afterwards a publisher of school-books; but has of late been in retirement from business.

Isaiah Thomas, the son of Isaiah Thomas, Jr., and grandson of Isaiah Thomas, the founder of this Society, was born in Worcester, Nov. 9, 1805; was fitted for college at Leicester Academy; graduated at Harvard College, in 1825. Soon after leaving college, he removed to Cincinnati, Ohio, and became one of the editors and publishers of the "Cincinnati American." He subsequently engaged in mercantile and agricultural pursuits. He, however, retained, during life, his ardent love of books, and was a constant writer for the press, as correspondent and critic. He was a rapid, easy, graceful writer; and every thing from his pen bore the marks of liberal and generous culture.

In the winter of 1862, under the statute authorizing the President to appoint salaried consuls for certain foreign ports, during the insurrection, he received from President Lincoln the appointment of Consul to Algiers. He sailed from New York for Havre, in February, 1862, in a merchant ship, with his daughter and two sons. The ship foundered probably a few days after leaving port; nothing was afterwards heard of ship or passengers or crew. Mr. Seward caused most thorough inquiries to be made; but no trace of the ship was ever discovered.

The Report of the Librarian, which accompanies and makes a part of the Report of the Council, shows that our Library, during the last six months, has received an unusual number of acquisitions. We are perhaps largely indebted for this to the increased interest which our recent valuable publications have excited.

The Report of the Treasurer is also quite satisfactory. It shows an increase in our several Funds, although the expenditures from each have been larger than usual; and also a small accumulation.

The Librarian's and General Fund amounts now to	$22,748.57
The Publishing Fund	7,206.25
The Fund for Collection and Research	9,828.38
And the Bookbinding Fund	7,353.35
Making an aggregate of	$47,136.55

all well invested.

While this Society has always interested itself specially in collecting the records of the past, it has recently been very fortunate in preserving those of the important present. To do this well is to perpetuate the memory of all that is valuable in our recent extraordinary experience as a nation. And the Council renewedly congratulate the Society in their possession of the valuable collections of newspapers and other ephemeral literature of the day; and especially of the remarkable volumes of extracts bearing upon the present civil war, and put together in historical order by their late lamented associate, Pickering Dodge. These will give the life of the present to the future student of history, representing the events of the day as they impress the people of the time. They are records of great movements of affairs, and also of their interior moral and political life. They present the development of the nation's resources, — the accumulating power, — the progress of ideas, — the century of life compressed into the history of the year. May we not hope that they will show to the future reader, also, how the war which is now consuming us is our fire of purification!

But there is before the Society no adequate record of the progress in science, in knowledge, and in civilization. It is for us to collect and preserve all that can illustrate this; that the history of this war may not be like that of other wars, a mere history of the progress of arms, and of conquest and subjugation, if such must be; but also a delineation of the development of the arts, and of acquisitions in science, of general enlightenment, and of social and political progress.

Such a collection should illustrate, not only progress in the art of war, in its destruction of human life and resources, and also the developments of knowledge and genius in their application to power and preservation, and so to the security of life, but also the rapid civilization, the large humanity, the cosmopolitan influences, which are the atmosphere of so large a war in this age.

The subject which opens before us under such a contemplation is so vast, that we can do no more than to call the attention of the Society to it, and to their duty as an association, in all that relates to history and progress. The history of war is, usually, little else but that of the movements of armies, with their great results. Details of military organization and of the disposition of troops are laid up in State Departments; but a great deal, even of that which concerns the preservation of armies, is lost; and, although social and political condition is changed, the moral history of this also is lost in the lustre and confusion of the military history.

It is remarkable that this should hold true, even as to what concerns the medical department of an army. The Director-General of the Army Medical Department of the British Army, in his report presented to Parliament in 1858, was obliged to say, that, in searching the records of his department, after a forty years' peace, " to ascertain what would probably be found necessary for the wants of the sick and wounded during a European war," he " found only two or three valueless documents, which merely indicated the number of staff medical officers serving in Spain during the few months of 1812." Here was more pomp than philanthropy. This poverty of record, so different from the fulness of statistics which characterizes all the French Departments, goes far towards explaining the disastrous inefficiency and unhappy inferiority which the British nation, always boastful of its practical virtue, manifested in all that concerned the preservation of human life in the Crimean war; an inferiority the more conspicuous because in daily contrast with the operations of the French in the same field, and a disaster so enormous as to have cost them more lives than the enemy's cannon. Their earlier and later statistics in this war, constituting material more proper for a medical paper than for a paper addressed to this association, read a lesson which must never be forgotten. The Medical Department of our own army, and the Sanitary Associations flowing out of the necessities of the times, have profited from it immensely; and it is to the collection and preservation of all that concerns matters of such moment that we call the attention of the Society now.

And we are proud to be able to state, that the Medical Department of our army, under its admirable organization, is keeping complete record of all that is valuable in medical experience, and in humanity, as applied to the preservation of life. Such contributions to science as are here treasured up cannot be too highly valued. We have already seen, in the experience of the British armies, how much suffering and loss the want of them entails.

The humanitarian experience of the Sanitary Commissions, and of all the associate philanthropic organizations, is a valuable complement of that of the War Department, and must not be lost.

The comparison of all this with what the world has known before is quite remarkable. We have no history of the medical department of armies in ancient times. Cyrus and Alexander and Cæsar are known, by occasional but very cursory allusion, to have had medical men with their armies; but their work was merely that of the treatment of wounds; and they were only χειρουργοι, or hand-workers. This was partly owing to the nature of warfare in their time, which, being mostly of single combat, involved multitudinous collision. It was also in part from the low grade of medical and surgical science. Enlightened pathology and hygiene, elucidating often proximate causes, which are all that science can reach, and involving the natural history of disease, are of comparatively modern investigation. Out from these steps prevention, which towers high above treatment. The French lost in the Crimean war twenty-four thousand five hundred and sixty-four men by disease, much of it of a preventable character, while they lost only three thousand eight hundred and forty by wounds; and the English lost, in about the same length of time, 16,297 by disease, and 1,761 by wounds. The Crimean Commission found the English army with a death-rate of sixty per cent per annum, which was afterwards reduced to one and one-seventh per cent. But Cyrus and Alexander and Cæsar left nothing that is valuable to us towards the preservation of human life; and military surgeons, even down to

Baron Larrey, continued to be little but hand-workers, and left nothing but treatises upon wounds, which are, after all, the least important part of military surgery. The higher sphere of sanitary care has only just been entered.

An army, in its vital aspect, is, in time of war, an aggregate of healthy and effective men, subject to unusual exposure. This is the theoretical condition, and should be the actual. The aggregation and the exposure are evils which we cannot avoid, but may modify. The management of these involves our science of prevention, and should be kept foremost in spite of the superstitious folly of the people, who clamor for "treatment," not recognizing that prevention should mostly supersede treatment, making it unnecessary. For men aggregated in large numbers and under restraint, air is the pabulum vitæ. Food makes blood; but air must purify it, or it is poison. This is the one essential element of military hygiene, the exponent of the medical lesson of the war; which we allude to, not as a medical fact only, but as a historical fact, not appreciated till of late, but abundantly proved by all our recent experience.[*]

---

[*] "Philadelphia Medical and Surgical Reporter," March 25, 1865, No. 421. State Medical Society of Illinois. Transactions of the meeting of 1864. Statistics of cases.

Mortality of Amputations of the Thigh.	Treated in Ordinary General-Hospital Buildings.	Treated in the Field, in good circumstances; viz., in Hut Hospitals, &c.
At the upper third	85 per cent	45 per cent.
At the middle third	60 „ „	30 „ „
At the lower third	30 „ „	20 „ „

Air — or, technically, ventilation — is the great preventive of disease in all aggregated life ; and what are called camp-diseases, under all their fatal names, are chiefly from the want of it. Exhalations, decomposition, putrefaction, miasmata, all are only air - poisons ; and cleanliness, also, is only personal ventilation.*

We dwell on this generalization because we deem it so important. To prevent disease in an army is not only a large humanity, but also the most economical and valuable system of keeping up its numbers ; for to allow hospitals to be filled with preventable disease is willingly to deprive an army of veteran and effective force, as well as to embarrass its movements. Of nearly one hundred and forty thousand patients in the hospitals in Constantinople, in the Crimean war, about one hundred and seventeen thousand were there for disease, mostly of a preventable character.

And we especially call attention to the importance

In the Mower Hospital, at Chestnut Hill, Philadelphia, where air is admitted freely to the wards, close to the head of each cot, so that the respiration is almost as pure as that of the open fields, out of six thousand patients no case of hospital gangrene has occurred ; only one death from erysipelas.

* The Russians, who have a national dread of fresh air, looking on it as a peril, allowed their patients at Simpheropol scarcely any ventilation. In February and March, 1856, they had here an average of over ten thousand patients, and a mortality of more than twenty per cent. At this same Mower General Hospital, in Philadelphia, up to May 1, 1864, nearly seven thousand patients had been treated, of which nearly three thousand were cases of gun-shot wounds. The mortality was two-thirds of one per cent. Also there had been only two cases of pyæmia. — " Transactions of American Medical Association," vol. xv. 1864.

of the preservation of all our experience here, because of its future value. The field is immense, and is crowded. The movements are rapid, and under excitement and confusion; and the history of all should be preserved. General Butler's practical treatise on yellow fever, at New Orleans, was the best the world has ever had. The multitude of an army is a multitude of facts, in a sanitary view, and evidence is accumulated and conclusive.

We have given as much space to this part of our subject as our scheme contemplated; and will only repeat, that the material bearing upon the sanitary history of the war, to the collection of which we urge, is the record of the systematic and extensive and efficient workings of the War Department under its surgical bureau; of the less formal and more ready operations of the Sanitary Commission, with their all-pervading ramifications; and of the separate organizations, in all the important towns, supported by local munificence. We would not neglect these last. The history of New England is typified in that of the " Mayflower ; " and the American Revolution may be read in the lives of the men of the town of Boston of that time.

We spoke also of the importance of the collection of all that can illustrate the progress in science, in knowledge, and in civilization, in this war.

Great acquisitions in science and in the arts are not likely to be lost. The little Monitor revolutionized naval warfare and naval architecture in an hour; and the lesson is learned. All masonry crumbles under American artillery, while earth-works stand, and may become even stronger; and Fort Sumter is a perpetual teacher.

But there are details peculiar to this war, and of rapid transition, whose collection and lesson should not be neglected. These are details of social and political development. They regard the various peoples concerned in the war,—those immediately acting in it,— those among whom it is carried on,— the loyal and the disloyal,— and the republican form of government, in its manifestation of strength as it bears upon the political status, the general condition, and the individual welfare, in times of special confusion and distress.

Here is material for the student of social and political science, without stint. The amalgamation of peoples under a fraternity of condition and danger, kindliness ripening into patriotism, and the Irishman and the German, in the same ditch, and under the same blanket with the native-born citizen, becoming Americans; the washing out of prejudices of section and of color; the general diffusion of an equal light; the aggregated power of a great people aroused to act in their strength,— are subjects of study, for which we may now gather material every day: so that the future student shall read anew, how war, which developes science and power, has a special potency for a new and large and crude people to amalgamate heterogeneous elements, to complete manhood, and to consolidate nationality.

The world moves by great marches. It is our peculiar province to mark the steps.

Report of the Treasurer.

The Treasurer of the American Antiquarian Society submits the following semi-annual Report, for the six months ending April 25, 1865:—

The Librarian's and General Fund, Oct. 20, 1864, was   . $22,044.04
     Received for dividends and interest since   .   .   .   1,630.74

           $23,674.78
     Paid for salaries and incidental expenses   .   .   926.21

     Present amount of this Fund   .   .   . $22,748.57

The Collection and Research Fund, Oct. 20, 1864, was   . $9,256.51
     Received for dividends and interest since   .   .   .   608.77

           $9,865.28
     Paid for incidental expenses   .   .   36.90

     Present amount of this Fund   .   .   9,828.38

The Bookbinding Fund, Oct. 20, 1864, was $6,967.75
     Received for dividends and interest since   .   .   .   410.10

           $7,377.85
     Paid for binding 24.50

     Present amount of this Fund,   .   .   7,353.35

The Publishing Fund, Oct. 20, 1864, was   .   .   . $7,096.14
     Received for dividends and interest since   .   .   298.54

           $7,394.68
     Paid for printing semi-annual Report and incidentals   188.43

     Present amount of this Fund   .   .   7,206.25

         Aggregate of the four Funds   .   .   . $47,136.55

Cash on hand, included in the foregoing statement   .   . $670.01

4

INVESTMENTS.

Librarian's and General Fund.

Worcester National Bank Stock	$1,800.00
City National Bank Stock (Worcester) . . .	100.00
Central National Bank Stock „ . . .	100.00
Citizens' National „ „ „ . . .	1,500.00
Quinsigamond „ „ „ . . .	2,300.00
Blackstone National Bank Stock (Uxbridge) . .	500.00
Oxford Bank Stock	400.00
Fitchburg Bank Stock	600.00
National Bank of Commerce Stock (Boston) . .	1,000.00
Shawmut National Bank „ „ . .	3,700.00
North National Bank „ „ . .	500.00
Massachusetts Bank „ „ . .	500.00
Worcester and Nashua Railroad Stock (37 shares) .	2,407.40
Northern (N.H.) Railroad Stock (12 shares) . .	615.00
United-States Five-twenty 6 per cent Bonds . .	1,500.00
United-States Ten-forty 5 per cent Bonds . . .	500.00
United-States Seven-thirty Bonds	1,300.00
United-States Certificate of Indebtedness . . .	2,021.64
Note	500.00
Cash	4.53
	$22,748.57

Collection and Research Fund.

Worcester National Bank Stock	$1,300.00
City National Bank Stock (Worcester) . . .	500.00
Oxford Bank Stock	200.00
National Bank of Commerce Stock (Boston) . .	800.00
National Bank of North America (Boston) . .	600.00
Webster Bank Stock (Boston)	800.00
Northern (N.H.) Railroad Stock (8 shares) . .	410.00
Norwich and Worcester Railroad Bond . . .	1000.00
United-States Five-twenty 6 per cent Bonds . .	3,800.00
United-States Seven-thirty Bonds	300.00
Cash	118.38
	9,828.38

Bookbinding Fund.

City National Bank Stock (Worcester) . . .	100.00
Quinsigamond Bank „ „ . . .	600.00
National Bank of Commerce Stock (Boston) . .	2,500.00
Webster Bank Stock (Boston)	2,500.00
Northern (N.H.) Railroad Stock (10 shares) . .	512.50
United-States Five-twenty 6 per cent Bonds . .	500.00
United-States Seven-thirty Bonds	400.00
Cash	240.85
	7,353.35

Amount carried forward . . $39,930.30

Publishing Fund.

Amount brought forward		$39,930.30
Central National Bank Stock (Worcester) .	$500.00	
Mechanics Bank Stock (Worcester) . . .	500.00	
Shawmut National Bank Stock (Boston) .	500.00	
Boston National Bank Stock	400.00	
Norwich and Worcester Railroad Bond. .	1,000.00	
United-States Five-twenty 6 per cent Bonds .	2,500.00	
United-States Seven-thirty Bonds . . .	1,000.00	
Note	500.00	
Cash	306.25	
		7,206.25
Total of the four Funds		$47,136.55

Respectfully submitted,   NATHANIEL PAINE,
                                        Treasurer of Am. Antiq. Society.

ANTIQUARIAN HALL, WORCESTER, April 25, 1865.

REPORT OF THE LIBRARIAN.

The accessions of the last six months have been varied and numerous. Some members of the Society have made large donations; many others have contributed valuable books or documents; and the general community have been frequent and liberal in their gifts.

Very soon after our last meeting, Frederic W. Paine, Esq. sent in a large number of substantial volumes; many of them important in character, and some of them rare. To these he has since made additions; the aggregate comprising one hundred and seventy-six books, seventeen pamphlets, and sundry minor memorials of passing history.

Hon. Isaac Davis has presented, at different times, the generous number, purposely rounded, of one thousand pamphlets, and one hundred books. Among the latter are copies of the New Testament in Sanscrit, Armenian, Bengali, Siamese, Chinese, and Oriya; the translation of Leicester Ambrose Sawyer; the corrected version of the American Bible Union; Rev. Dr.

Conant's translation of the Book of Job; and the reprint of Roger Williams's " Experiments of Spiritual Life and Health." Religious, philanthropical, and denominational publications are also largely represented among his pamphlets.

From Hon. Levi Lincoln, we have received one hundred and two miscellaneous pamphlets, the " National Intelligencer" for 1864, in continuation, and the papers printed at the Sailors' Fair in Boston.

Stephen Salisbury, jr., Esq., has presented seventy-nine numbers of periodicals, and the " London Illustrated News," in continuation.

Hon. John G. Palfrey, Hon. Emory Washburn, Dr. James H. Salisbury, Professor James Davie Butler, Hon. Benjamin F. Thomas, Hon. William Willis, Hon. Charles Hudson, Hon. Robert C. Winthrop, and Don Jose F. Ramirez, members of the Society, have presented publications of their own authorship. Among these are the third volume of Dr. Palfrey's " History of New England," — the completion (temporarily, at least) of another great American work, to increase the distinction our country has won in that department of literature; — and the second edition, revised and enlarged, of Mr. Willis's elaborate and able history of Portland, beautifully printed, and largely illustrated. Accompanying this was a copy of the reprint, with additions, of the first volume of the Collections of the Maine Historical Society, to which Mr. Willis had been a principal contributor.

Hon. Charles Hudson has deposited a highly interesting manuscript memorial, from his own private and personal information, of the political life and services of Hon. John Davis, late President of the Society. Pliny E. Chase, Esq., has transmitted from Philadelphia a paper on the unitary origin of language, illustrated by a comparison of American languages with some of the early dialects of the Eastern Hemisphere. Commodore George S. Blake, to whom the Society was recently indebted for two beautifully executed drawings of Dighton Rock, made by the drawing-master and the chaplain of the Naval School at Newport, under his charge, has now forwarded a learned essay on that interesting monument, and the associations that have been connected with it, by Rev. Charles R. Hale, the chaplain of the Naval School. This manuscript is elaborately and ingeniously illustrated, and is handsomely bound for preservation in our library. The painting of the rock, and the full-sized delineation of the inscription, presented by Rev. Edward E. Hale at the meeting of the Society in October, also belong properly to this report, although mentioned in the *Proceedings* already printed. Rev. Dr. Alonzo Hill has deposited manuscripts of Rev. Stephen Bemis, a former minister of some note in the town of Harvard.

Other members of the Society, not already mentioned, have made valuable donations to the library ; viz., Dr. Nathaniel B. Shurtleff, Hon. John P. Bige-

low, Joel Munsell, Esq., Rev. Dr. Seth Sweetzer,
Hon. Ira M. Barton, Hon. Charles Sumner, Major L.
A. Huguet Latour, Hon. Stephen Salisbury, George
Livermore, Esq., Dr. Edward Jarvis, Dr. George Chan-
dler, Professor Edward Tuckerman, Dr. Joseph Sar-
gent, Nathaniel Paine, Esq., William A. Whitehead,
Esq., Hon. Ebenezer Torrey.

The full record of donors and donations is deferred
to a later portion of the Report.

Among the books recently received is a volume of
five hundred and twelve pages, bearing this title,
" Memorial Volume of the Popham Celebration,
August 29, 1862, commemorative of the Planting of
the Popham Colony on the Peninsula of Sabino,
August 19, O.S., 1607, establishing the Title of England to the Continent."

It is the record of an effort on the part of the Historical Society of Maine to substantiate certain new
views relating to the possession and settlement of this
continent; and to perpetuate their recognition by the
most formal and solemn proceedings, and by durable
monuments and inscriptions.

It may be expected that other Historical Societies,
and especially the American Antiquarian Society, will
give to these claims so much attention as shall be
necessary to determine how far they are entitled to
general acceptance.

The ceremonies described in the " Memorial Volume " were of the most elaborate and impressive

character; embracing the co-operation of not only the civil and judicial authorities of that State, and the representatives of its literature and science, but the learned associations and distinguished men of other States and the British Provinces, and even the General Government of the country. Each element of the pageant had its special part to perform; and the influence of each was made .to bear upon the great object of the gathering. It is, therefore, of no little historical consequence to understand distinctly what it was proposed to accomplish on that occasion, and the manner in which the purpose was effected.

We are informed, that, in the arrangements made by the Government of the United States for the defence of Maine, a point of land near the mouth of the Kennebec was selected for a fort; and that near the spot thus chosen was the site of the ancient Fort St. George; " where, in the month of August, 1607, the first English colony, led by the venerable George Popham, planted the emblems of the authority of their sovereign. By acts of formal occupation and possession, attended with the solemn sanction of religious worship and instruction, in accordance with the usages of their country and time, these early settlers established the title of England to the continent, under the Royal Charter of April 10, 1606."

The Commissioners of the State on the subject of Coast Defences having suggested to the General Government the name of Popham as a suitable designation for the fort, the proposal was approved; and that name was adopted by direction of the Secretary of War.

The idea was then conceived of " reviving the recollection of the important events which have given to the spot its great historical value and interest, and of connecting them more closely with the name and destinies of the fortification; thus making it serve the double purpose of national defence, and the preservation of those leading occurrences of our early history." Measures were therefore adopted for erecting, in the walls of the fort, a " Memorial Stone," with inscriptions recording the facts, and for the commemorative services of a public historical celebration.

A stone was prepared, to be placed in the walls of the fort by the officer representing the United-States Government, which contained an inscription, " proclaiming," says the orator of the day, "to future times, in the simple eloquence of truthful words, that —

> 'THE FIRST COLONY
> ON THE SHORES OF NEW ENGLAND
> Was Founded Here,
> August 19th, O.S., 1607,
> Under
> GEORGE POPHAM.' "

As a companion to this outward monument, a tablet was provided by the Historical Society for the interior of the structure, with a Latin inscription in honor of George Popham. The first portion of the Society's translation of this reads thus: —

" In Memory of
GEORGE POPHAM,
Who first, from the shores of England,
Founded a Colony in New England,
August, 1607.
He brought into these wilds
English laws and learning,
And the faith and the Church of Christ."

" This fort," declares the orator, " so conspicuously placed, bearing these appropriate testimonials, thus becomes a fitting monument to perpetuate the events of the early history of New England, and transmit to future times the memory of those illustrious men who laid the foundation of English colonies in America."

These statements, as may be supposed, were repeated in various forms, and enlarged upon, in the course of the proceedings recorded in the " Memorial Volume."

At the time appointed for the celebration, the marshal of the day announced the purpose and plan of the ceremonies, as intended to recall and illustrate the events of the past, and to assign to Maine her true historic position.

The Bishop of the Diocese then proceeded to the religious duties of the occasion; using, we are told, as nearly as the changed circumstances of the case would allow, " the same services as were employed by the colonists in their solemnities on the day commemorated, under the guidance of their chaplain, the Rev. Richard Seymour."

These services, from the Episcopal Prayer-book, were followed by a narrative of historical events by the President of the Historical Society.

The "Memorial Stone" was then rolled forward into view, — a mass of granite weighing six tons, and showing a front of six feet by four; and the President of Bowdoin College solicited the consent of the State and General Government to its being placed in the wall of the fort, " in memory of the colony which was established there two hundred and fifty-five years ago," — " that noble company of one hundred and twenty colonists who established themselves at the mouth of the Sagadahoc."

Hon. Abner Coburn responded on behalf of the Governor of the State ; and Captain Casey, of the United-States Bureau of Engineers, gave the assent of the President, acting through the Secretary of War. The President of the College next called upon the Freemasons to cause the stone to be erected according to the ancient rites of their Order.

After these solemnities, the orator of the day delivered his address ; which was followed by a series of sentiments and speeches, and the reading of letters, at the table.

The toasts had been previously printed, and were published and circulated beforehand, with the programme of the exercises; having been framed with deliberation, and carefully adjusted to the purposes of the occasion. Among the earliest were these : —

"The 19th of August (O.S.), 1607, — ever memorable as the day that witnessed the consummation of the title of England to the New World."

"The memory of George Popham, who led hither the first English Colony, became the head of its government, &c., and left his bones to mingle with the soil," &c.

"Sir John Popham, — under the shadow of whose great name was laid the foundation of the colossal Empire of the New World."

Far down, below the salt, we find [the twenty-seventh toast] —

"Plymouth Plantation, — founded by men of strong faith, of earnest piety. Educated under the teachings of Robinson and Brewster at Leyden, they were fitted to become pioneers in the new movement towards civil and religious liberty."

Two steps farther down, we have —

"The Colony of Massachusetts Bay, — founded, in 1629, by men of the same unconquerable will as those that brought royalty to the block, and discarded prescription as heresy. Their descendants have ever shown a faithful adherence to the doctrine of 'Uniformity.'" *

The address of the orator of the day is an endeavor to maintain, argumentatively and rhetorically, the points assumed in the preceding quotations. It contains many quite extraordinary historical statements, which are not necessary to be reproduced here, as

---

* Ex-Governor Washburn, of Massachusetts, was called upon to respond to this toast; and, after good-naturedly intimating his surprise at some of the points which had been assumed, confessed that he had been utterly disarmed by the courtesies he had shared, and would no longer protest against any thing; and if anybody were to insist that Noah's Ark landed on one of those hills, and would get up a celebration like that to commemorate it, he would volunteer to come and take a part in it, without doubting it was true.

they have but a remote bearing on the principal questions. It begins thus: —

"We commemorate to-day the great event of American history. We are assembled on the spot that witnessed the first formal act of possession of New England by a British colony, under the authority of a Royal Charter. We have come here, on the two hundred and fifty-fifth anniversary of that event, to rejoice in the manifold blessings that have flowed to us from that act ; to place on record a testimonial of our appreciation of that day's work ; and to transmit to future generations an expression of our regard for the illustrious men who laid the foundation of England's title to the Continent, and gave a new direction to the history of the world."

The argument is, in brief, as follows: —

"The question Europeans were called upon to solve at the commencement of the seventeenth century was, who should hereafter occupy and possess the temperate zone of the New World? All previous explorations were preliminary efforts to this object ; but the question remained open and undecided.

" England, practically abandoning all claims from the discoveries of Cabot on the Atlantic, and Drake on the Pacific, laid down, in 1580, the broad doctrine, that prescription without occupation was of no avail ; that possession of the country was essential to the maintenance of title.

" The possession of Newfoundland by Sir Humphrey Gilbert was abandoned on his loss at sea.

" Of the two colonies sent out by Sir Walter Raleigh, one returned ; the other perished in the country, leaving no trace of its history.

" Thus, at the period of Elizabeth's death in 1603, England had not a colonial possession on the globe.

" Champlain accompanied Pont Gravé to the St. Lawrence in 1603. On his return to France, he found Acadia granted by the French monarch to De Monts, under date of Nov. 8, 1603, extending across the continent between the fortieth and forty-sixth degrees of north latitude. To make sure of the country, Champlain, Champdore, and L'Escarbot remained three and a half years. Returning to France in 1607, they found the charter of De Monts revoked.

"This short-sightedness of Henry of Navarre cost France the dominion of the New World.

"For, in 1605, Gorges, associating with himself the Earl of Southampton, petitioned the king for a charter, which he obtained April 10, 1606, granting to George Popham and seven others" (it should be Sir Thomas Gates and seven others; Popham is the last named) "the Continent of North America, from the thirty-fourth to the forty-fifth degrees of north latitude.

"This charter is the basis on which rests the title of our race to the New World.

"The venerable Sir John Popham became the patron of the company, . . . though his name was not in the charter, or included among the council.

"Two unsuccessful attempts at planting a colony were made in 1606. On the 31st of May, 1607, the first colony to New England sailed from Plymouth for the Sagadahoc, in two ships, the 'Gift of God,' George Popham commander, and the 'Mary and John,' commanded by Raleigh Gilbert, on board which ships were one hundred and twenty persons for planters. On the 19th of August, all went on shore at the mouth of the river, where they had a sermon from their preacher; the President's commission was read, with the patent, and the laws to be observed; and George Popham was nominated President, &c.

"Thus commenced the first occupation and settlement of New England. From August 10 (O.S.), 1607, the title of England to the New World was maintained.

"It is well known, that the Popham Colony, or a portion of them, returned to England in 1608; but this possession proved sufficient to establish the title. The revocation of the charter of De Monts gave priority to the grant of King James, covering the same territory; and this formal act of possession was ever after upheld by an assertion of the title by Gorges."

The orator repeats, that England stoutly maintained, that, without possession, there was no valid title to a newly-discovered country. "This view," he says, "is overlooked by Puritan writers, and those who follow their authority." He does not tell us how it happened, if priority of discovery by the Cabots, and formal acts of possession by Gilbert, Gosnold, and others, established no rights, the British Government could convey any title, by charter, to a country already occupied by the subjects of other powers.

The only allusions to the colony of Gosnold and the settlement of Jamestown are where he claims that Gorges was concerned in the voyage of Gosnold, and in the following passages: —

"It may be said, that, in giving this prominence to the occupation of the country by the colony of Popham, we overlook other events of importance in establishing the English title, — the possession of the Elisabeth Isles by Gosnold in 1602, and the settlement of Jamestown, May 13, 1607, prior to the landing of the Popham colony at Sagadahoc.

"In reference to the occupation of Elizabeth Isles by Gosnold, it is sufficient to say, that it was prior to the date of the Royal Charter, and consequently of no legal effect in establishing a title. As to the settlement of Jamestown, it was south of the fortieth parallel of latitude, and therefore did not come in conflict with the French king's prior charter to De Monts.

"Had there been no English settlement or occupancy north of the fortieth parallel of latitude prior to 1610, when Poutrincourt obtained a new grant of Acadia, the whole country north of that line must have fallen into the hands of the French." *

---

* It is understood, that these paragraphs, referring to the colony of Gosnold and the settlement of Jamestown, were inserted after the address was delivered.

There is no sufficient opportunity here for a discussion of these propositions; but it may be instructive to place beside them, in the briefest terms, a different statement, believed to be at least equally well sanctioned by the best historical evidence.

It is due to the venerable and learned President of the Maine Historical Society to quote from his excellent remarks a passage which is overshadowed by the great mass of opposite sentiment expressed in the "Memorial Volume." Speaking of the Popham settlement, he says, "But, sir, the enterprise failed: death and the stars seemed against it; and there were 'no more speeches' by the Northern Company, says Gorges, 'of settling any other plantation in those parts for a long time after.' They were in search of gain, and found it not in peopling a rude continent. It was essentially a commercial company: the principle that moved it was adverse to generous action; it required another sentiment, the religious element, to give patient endurance, indomitable resolution, and final success, as was signally vindicated in the renowned colony of the Pilgrims. The Northern Company made no other attempt at colonization, until they obtained their charter of 1620. We must not claim too much for this unsuccessful attempt to people a continent, but regard it as *one* of the steps in the grand march of colonization."

It could hardly be expected, that the learned President would enter a more emphatic protest against the extravagant claims which persons of less accurate information were disposed to advance, or that he would dwell upon circumstances not in harmony with the general spirit of the occasion ; but it may be permitted to others to say, in the cause of historical truth, and in accordance with the most authentic recorded testimony, —

First, That the official act of possession, by Sir Humphrey Gilbert in 1583, made in virtue of the original discovery by the Cabots, was of the most formal and perfect character. It was conducted with all prescribed ceremonies for such procedures, in the presence of representatives of every prominent antagonistic power, — the numerous merchants and masters of vessels engaged in the fisheries, — whose assent was signified by loud acclamations, by the acceptance of grants of land, and by consent to taxation ; for the English had, before that time, been regarded as " lords of the harbors," and had exacted a tribute for protection afforded to the ships of other nations. So far from being abandoned on the death of Gilbert, the British sovereignty was enforced, two years later, by the seizure of Portuguese vessels, which had collected cargoes without a license ; and it is stated, that, about the year 1600, the English employed at Newfoundland, on land and water, quite ten thousand men and boys.*

---

* Sabine's Report.

Second, That De Monts took possession of Acadia, not in his own name, but as lieutenant-general of the French king, on whose behalf he set up the arms and insignia of France. The revocation, alleged to be an abandonment or invalidation of the French title, was merely the withdrawal of certain exclusive privileges which had been granted to De Monts for ten years; while the acts of possession and colonization were continued and enlarged by the French monarch. The respective rights of the English and French to the possession of New England or of Canada were not settled by a comparison of dates, or the construction of charters, but by the valor of the Massachusetts colony, the force of arms, and subsequent treaties.

Third, That the revival of plans of colonization, and their direction to New England, were the results of the voyage of Gosnold in 1602; when he came with a colony for settlement, and, having traversed the coast of Maine, built a fort, and planted grain at Cuttyhunk, on the south shore of Massachusetts. From the fear of inadequate supplies, on the part of his men, he subsequently carried them back to England, where, by his glowing description of the country and his personal exertions, he was instrumental in the procurement of the great Virginia patent of 1606.

Fourth, That the scheme of a plantation at Sagadahoc originated with the kidnapping of Indians

from that neighborhood by Weymouth in 1605; three
of whom came into the possession of Sir Ferdinando
Gorges, the projector of the plan, who says it was
suggested by information derived from these natives.
Chief-Justice Popham, the patron of the undertaking,
was reported to be " the first person who invented
the plan of sending convicts to the plantations,"—
which is not precisely true, for the French colonists,
under La Roche and De Monts, had been chiefly
composed of convicts from the prisons. But it is
said of Popham, that " he not only punished male-
factors, but provided for them; and first set up the
discovery of *New* England to maintain and employ
those that could not live honestly in the *Old*." Sir
William Alexander, a contemporary witness, testifies
that Sir John Popham " sent out the first company
that went of purpose to inhabit there, near to Sagadahoc: but those that went thither being pressed to that
enterprise as endangered by the law, or for their own
necessities,—no enforced thing being pleasant,—they,
after a winter's stay, dreaming to themselves of new
hopes at home, returned back with the first occasion;
and, to justify the suddennesse of their returne, they
did coyne many excuses, burdening the bounds where
they had beene with all the aspersions they could
possibly devise; seeking by that meanes to discourage
all others."*

---

* The orator at the Maine celebration quotes from Sir William Alexander
the statement, that " Sir John Popham sent out the first company that went

Fifth, That this company, of *one hundred* landmen
or colonists according to Gorges, so constituted, had
with them several men of standing, as leaders. In-
deed, such was the case with every similar enterprise
at that period; and especially just then, when the
termination of war with Spain threw large numbers of land and sea-officers out of employment.
They selected a place near the mouth of the Kennebec or Sagadahoc, as it was then called, where they
built a fort or stockade, and storehouses and habita-
tions. More than half of the company are said to
have gone back with the ships in December. The
residue, forty-five in number, remained till spring;
when, having lost their leader, having quarrelled with
the Indians, and had their storehouses burned, they
took the first opportunity to leave the country, and
gave it so bad a name as to discourage all further
attempts at settlement. The business of fishing and
traffic with the natives, which had existed on the coasts
for nearly a century, was continued, with only such
casual occupation of the land as that business re-

---

of purpose to inhabit there, near to Sagadahoc," but carefully suppresses the
remainder of the passage.

Another remarkable suppression in the "Memorial Volume" is that of the
speech of our associate, J. W. Thornton, Esq., made by invitation in reply to
a toast at the table. Mr. Thornton's views of the Maine Colony, and the
characters of Gorges and Chief-Justice Popham, were not satisfactory to the
Committee having charge of the celebration, and were therefore omitted from
their narrative of the proceedings. The speech has since been published by
the author, with copious and learned notes, sustaining his positions, and full
of minute and curious information relating to colonial history.

quired. * Captain John Smith relates, that, when
(about 1614) he went first to the part of the country
where this colony had been planted, there was not one
Christian in all the land ; and yet Newfoundland at
that time freighted annually near eight hundred ships
with fish. The very place where Popham's company
passed the winter was forgotten, and was a subject of
conjecture and controversy until 1849, when the
Hakluyt Society of England published, from a newly
discovered manuscript, " The Historie of Travaile into
Virginia Britannia," by William Strachey, who had
been employed as Secretary in the Southern Colony.

That history contains the only particular account
of the expedition of Popham's company, and fixes the
spot where they passed the winter. It has not a
word about any ceremonies used to signify taking
possession of the country; not a word about Episcopal services, or the reading of prayers, or liturgy, or
any ritual of the Church, even at the burial of their
chief. The writer was led to speak of the enterprise,
" since it had its end so untimely," and since the order
and method of a full history did claim of him " the
remembrance of the most material points at least, as
well of this late Northern Colony, as of the first planted
more south." He closes his narrative by saying,

---

* There is an effort in the "Memorial Volume" to make it appear proba-
ble that a portion of Popham's men remained in the country. It would not
have been strange, if some of them had found employment among the fishing
vessels ; but Strachey says they *all* embarked for home.

" And this was the end of that Northern Colony upon the river Sagadahoc."

If the discovery by the Cabots, and the elaborate acts of occupation and jurisdiction by Sir Humphrey Gilbert, as the direct representative of his sovereign, — subsequently enforced and sustained, — created no permanent rights; if the colonies of Raleigh, the last of which, if it perished, at least left its bones on the soil, planted no durable claims; if Gosnold, who was not only the first Englishman, but the first European, who is known to have set up a dwelling on the soil of New England; who had been sent by the Earl of Southampton for the purpose of continuing Raleigh's plans of colonization; who gave names to islands and capes on our coast, which they still retain; whose particular narratives, thrice told, revived the sinking hopes of the friends of colonization, and whose personal efforts brought about the great revival of such enterprises in 1606, — if all these gave no valid possession to the British crown, how can this evanescent company of Sagadahoc, with all its failures and all its injurious influence, be said to have " established the title of England to the continent"? It did not even establish itself, or leave a distinguishable memorial behind it. What could there be in the charter of 1606 to give to feebler demonstrations an efficiency which equally solemn grants from the same source did not impart to greater and more persistent procedures?

The orator of the day, towards the close of his address, thought proper to allude to Massachusetts in a manner that explains the somewhat ambiguous toast which has already been quoted. He says, —

"We must not forget our obligations to Massachusetts and the early settlers of Plymouth for their share in conquering the continent for our race, though dealing harshly with Maine. Those Massachusetts Puritans of the Saxon type, inheriting all the gloomy errors of a cruel and bloody period under the iron rule of the Tudors, were ready to demand of Elizabeth the enforcement of the Act of Uniformity against the Papists, but refused obedience to it themselves."

Among similar passages, he declares, " They mistook their hatred of others for hatred of sin. They set up their own morbid convictions as the standard of right." — " Once planted on the shores of New England, the Puritans of Massachusetts Bay endeavored to exterminate every thing that stood in the way of their ambition," &c., &c.

Accompanying the records of the Popham celebration is a lecture, by the author of the address, on the claims of Sir Ferdinando Gorges as the Father of English Colonization in America. This had previously been delivered before the Historical Societies of Maine and New York, and now makes a part of the " Memorial Volume."

A large portion of the lecture is in a strain

resembling that of the extracts taken from the address, but more acrid and bitter.

"It is time," the author thinks, " to vindicate the truth of history; to do justice to the claims of Gorges, and to repel the calumnious charges of the men who founded the theocracy of New-England ; who persecuted alike Quakers, Baptists, and Churchmen." " Within the boundaries of the Colony of Massachusetts Bay, from the time they first landed till the arrival of Sir Edmund Andros, as Governor, in 1686, the Government of Massachusetts Bay was more arbitrary and intolerant than any despotism from which they fled from England." — " The modern popular history of New England has sought to conceal the exact truth, and to throw apology over the greatest offences." — " We find the Massachusetts Puritans persecutors from the outset of their career ; denying the rights of citizenship to all but actual church members, and refusing others protection even against the Indians." Mr. Webster's great speech at Plymouth, in 1820, he calls an Epic Poem, in which the truth of severe history has been overlooked in admiration of the creations of his genius. Mr. Everett follows the authority of Mr. Webster ; and " modern historians have since then taken these flights of poetic fancy for historic verities, and sought to elevate them into the dignity of history. They might as well insist, that a modern Fourth-of-July oration was the cause of the Revolutionary War, though uttered some years after that event had taken place. Regarded as a political event, the Plymouth settlement was not of the slightest consequence or importance. It neither aided nor retarded the settlement of the country."

These are all the specimens for which time or space can now be afforded, though they inadequately represent the tone and spirit of the lecture. We may be permitted to present, by way of rejoinder, a few "historic verities," which could easily be sustained by proof.

First, It is fortunate for Maine, and for the country, that New England was not peopled by the convict and mercenary gangs of Gorges. It would have been well, also, perhaps, if the Pilgrims had remained a year or two longer in Holland. For the colony at Jamestown, composed of like unsound materials, was apparently near its end, perishing from its inherent vices, and might have been re-established by better men, under better auspices. Gorges himself discloses the fact of his own utter discouragement. But the proposed embarkation of the Pilgrims changed all that, and infused new life into the dying hopes of speculators in the anticipated resources of the New World. Gorges eagerly seized the opportunity of planting permanent occupants on the soil; which, he tells us, all his efforts had failed to accomplish. He favored the plans of the emigrants to Plymouth, and

7

of the company of Massachusetts Bay, until he found that they would not be made to subserve his private and selfish purposes, when he turned against them, and sought to deprive them of their rights and privileges.

Second, The arrival of the Pilgrims at Plymouth was the transfer to this country of an actual community, possessing all the important relations of domestic life. It was like transplanting a tree with roots already formed, and tendrils already grown, to take hold of the new soil, and maintain vitality, even if all above them perished. Hence neither suffering nor death could break up the colony, because here was its home, and it had no other.

The Massachusetts Company was a body politic. Having brought its charter, it became a State or Commonwealth, dependent on no corporation or council on the other side of the ocean, but sufficient of itself for all the purposes of human society. It proceeded immediately to build up towns and municipalities after the hereditary patterns of the mother-country; to organize government and the administration of law and justice in all the customary branches; to establish commerce; to found seats of learning, and create an army of drilled and disciplined soldiers. It was an integral portion of England that was thus removed to America, comprising some of its most learned scholars and ablest divines; some of its wisest and shrewdest politicians; some of its most sagacious merchants; and some well skilled in the arts of war. So rapid and substantial was the progress in the first seven years of occupation, that the jealousy of England was excited, and emigration was restrained. For, says Gorges, "it was doubted that they would in a short time wholly shake off the royal jurisdiction of the sovereign magistrate." It was at this period that the General Court of Massachusetts passed an order, that none should be received to inhabit within its jurisdiction, without liberty from one of the standing council, or two other assistants. "They were of opinion," says Holmes, "that their Commonwealth was established by free consent; that the place of their habitation was their own; that no man had a right to enter their society without their permission; that they had the full and absolute power of governing all people by men chosen from among themselves, and according to such laws as they should see fit to make, not repugnant to the laws of England." They were able, a very few years later, to furnish statesmen, warriors, and preachers, who contributed materially to the conversion of the English Government into a Commonwealth.

Thus were first fulfilled, beyond the chances of controversy, the conditions of the doctrine laid down in the "Memorial Volume," that prescription without occupation was of no avail, and that possession of the country was essential to the maintenance of title. The success of Massachusetts made possible the possession and settlement of other portions of the northern continent. Her vigor encouraged, and her commercial intercourse animated, every other colony. Without her protection, even in later times, every plantation in Maine would probably have been destroyed by the Indians, certainly would have been overwhelmed by the French; and even the older settlements of Virginia apparently owed their continued existence to the prosperity of New England. Nor would the stronger company of Massachusetts Bay have come into existence except for the pioneer enterprise of the Pilgrims.

Third, No sooner had Plymouth and Massachusetts established the practicability of living and thriving in New England, than, in addition to the lawless adventurers who already frequented the coasts, the country began to swarm with outcasts of every description. They were not unlike the miscellaneous characters which, in our own time, first poured into California; persons who, if not actually vicious, were of roving and restless natures, and impatient of the restraints of society. The religious agitations of the period had also set afloat other classes equally dangerous to the peace of a community: visionaries and fanatics of every genus, — Familists, Fifth-monarchy men, Antinomians, Anabaptists, Quakers; some of them under respectable names, which then covered entirely different pretensions and practices. There were men who disdained obedience to laws, or conformity to the ordinary rules of social life; and women who thought it their duty to prophesy in public, to vilify the magistrates, and to parade the streets in a state of nudity. A nation strengthened by the growth of centuries might possibly withstand the influence of such disorganizing elements; but, without restraints almost as rigorous as martial law, they would seem to be necessarily fatal to the safety of an infant colony.

The Puritans were not fanatics, of the visionary kind at least, but with earnest piety mingled worldly wisdom. They asserted the broad distinction between imposing restrictions upon the liberties of established communities inheriting the soil from a common ancestry, and defining the conditions of admission to their own religious and political fellowship, in a new land, bought with their money, planted by their toil, and watered with their tears. A candid and philosophical discussion of the whole subject, between Winthrop and Vane, has fortunately been preserved to us, and shows the solemn deliberation with which their policy was adopted.*

Fourth, Those practices and municipal regulations which are so much decried as novel persecutions, or as evidences of bigotry and narrow-mindedness peculiar to New England, did not originate here. They were not even of Puritan origin. They were trans-

---

* Hutchinson's " Collection of Original Papers."

ferred from the local statute-books of their English homes, where they had been familiar to the people for generations. In many of the ancient towns of England, precisely similar enactments were in force. Persons were carted about town, and then "expulsed," simply for eaves-dropping. If a man spoke evil of the magistrates, he was to be grievously punished in his body; and, if he struck the Mayor, was to lose the offending hand. At Leicester, one person from every house was required to be at every sermon. At Boston, in 1616, all the street-doors were to be kept closed during divine service; and in 1662 the council ordered, that every person in the borough above twenty-one years of age should "diligently and faithfully attend divine service upon every Sunday, or other days of thanksgiving and humiliation appointed by law." The Wardens of Childwal, in 1635, presented individuals who absented themselves from the parish church, or who slept during service. At Liverpool, people were punished for lodging guests who did not go to church. At the same place, a minister was threatened with punishment for not cutting his hair to a seemly length; and it was declared illegal for a bachelor to be out in the street after nine o'clock, P.M. At Hartlepool, any member of the corporation was fined for sitting out of his regular place at church. At Lancaster, strangers were prohibited from coming into town until they had permission from the Mayor, his brethren, and fifteen commons. At

Banbury, the people could not receive an inmate or under-tenant without license from the Mayor. If, without license, they kept a visitor thirteen days, they were fined forty shillings, and lost the freedom of the town. At Leicester, in 1564, no townsmen could sit and tipple at an alehouse, but must take the beer to their own houses.

The Puritans of New England, to meet the exigencies of their colony, simply continued a class of municipal rules to which they were habituated in the mother-country. Perhaps they should have been wiser than their fathers in this respect, as they were in some others. Perhaps their policy was required by the circumstances in which they were placed. It would be presumptuous in us to pronounce, that a different course would have produced more favorable results. They were men of remarkable common sense and practical ability: as Bishop Warburton said, they *had a genius for government.* They also believed in the necessity of law.

One of the toasts at the Maine celebration was framed to compliment the " tolerant spirit " of the Dutch of Manhattan, as contrasted with the *intolerant* spirit of New England; and the New-York gentleman who responded in advance by letter indulged in a similar tone of remark. Among statements, not so well founded as they should be, coming from so respectable a source, two contiguous passages are selected for illustration : —

" If the pioneer settlement at New Plymouth was distinguished from the later colony of Massachusetts Bay by more tolerant ideas in civil as well as religious affairs, it may be not unjustly inferred, that some, at least, of that larger liberality was derived from the lessons of Holland."

" Meanwhile, the Dutch colonists at Manhattan, and its neighborhood, had been calmly practising those liberal principles which they learned in their fatherland. There the Jesuit Father Jogues met Protestant exiles from the persecutions of Massachusetts, Lutherans from Germany, Roman Catholics and Anabaptists, all actually enjoying, in an equal degree with the original Calvinistic settlers, the blessings of religious liberty."

The first book we happen to take up for light on this subject is Mr. Onderdonk's " Queen's County in Olden Times; " and it does not appear from his minutes, that Baptists, or Quakers, or other schismatics, were treated more leniently by the Dutch, under similar circumstances, than they were by the Puritans of Massachusetts and Connecticut.

" 1656. Wm. Wickendam, a cobler from Rhode Island, came to Flushing and began to preach, and went with the people into the river, and dipped them. For this he was fined £100, and ordered to be banished. As he was poor and had a family, the fine was remitted. Hallet, the sheriff, had dared to collect conventicles in his house, and had permitted Wickendam to preach and administer the sacraments, though not called thereto by any ecclesiastical authority. For this he was removed from office, and fined £50."

The next year, Wickendam began to preach and baptize again.

" This becoming known to the Governor, the Fiscaal proceeded to Flushing, and brought him along. He was banished the Province."

"1661, July 4. Thos. Terry and Saml. Dearing petition for leave to settle seven families at Hempstead, [and] ten at Matinecook. Granted; but they are to bring in no Quakers, or such like *opinionists*"!!

"1670. The people of Jamaica petition the Governor against a certain witch, Katherine Harison's settling there. Petition granted." She had been sent away from Connecticut.

"1674, April 18. Samuel Furman, of Oysterbay, went about the streets of New York making a great noise and uproar, and presumed to come into the Church and abuse the word of God, and blaspheme his holy name; for which he is sentenced to be severely whipped with rods, banished the Province, and pay the costs."

Perhaps some who have since borne the respectable name of Furman on Long Island could have told us whether the blasphemy in this case differed from that generally charged upon religious enthusiasts of the ranting order, then so common and troublesome.

"1674, Nov. 24. Daniel Patrick and Francis Coley, of Flushing, for contemptuously working on Thanksgiving Day, and giving reproachful language to the magistrates that questioned them for it, are sent to the New York Sessions by Justice Cornell and Mr. Hinchman."

"1675. Thomas Case, while preaching at Matinecook, is arrested by the constable of Oysterbay."

"1675, Oct. Mary Case is fined £5 for interrupting Mr. Leverich while preaching, and saying to him, 'Come down, thou whited wall, thou that feedest thyself, and starvest the people!' The constable led her out of the meeting. Samuel Scudder is fined £5, or go to jail, for sending a long and scandalous letter to Mr. Leverich. Francis Coely submits, and is dismissed. Elizabeth Appleby disturbed the Court of Sessions, and is committed. Thomas Case is fined £20 for preaching and making a disturbance before John Brown's door at Flushing."

Thomas Case was a Quaker, who had some peculiar notions on the subject of marriage. Under date of Jan. 12, 1676, it is said, "Too many persons visit Thomas Case in prison. None hereafter to be admitted." He was a pestilent fellow, no doubt, yet seems to have been popular.

But where are we? Among the "tolerant" Knickerbockers, or the bigoted Puritans? Do practices change their nature and their name according to the localities in which they occur? It has been the misfortune of the Maine celebration to involve, not only its managers, but some of its invited guests, in a singular confusion of ideas respecting "historic verities."

The sneers at Puritanism, so common in the Southern States, may have arisen partly from jealousy, and partly from a natural incapacity to conceive of habits of life and conduct, restrained or impelled by abstract principles of right and duty. But the imitative echo, sometimes heard from the great commercial metropolis, when repeated in Maine, has the derogatory elements of ingratitude and questionable taste. For the people of that State are not descended from Popham's *cavaliers*, nor from the remains of a subjected colony, but are indebted to Massachusetts for the being of their commonwealth, and the guardianship of its defenceless years.

In passing judgment upon the authors of great movements in the world's history, it is not customary to dwell on their minor traits, even if these are faults, but on those characteristics which overcame obstacles and secured success; and never, before or since, has the conquest of a country been effected with so little of public wrong or private injustice as that of the land which we inhabit, whether we regard the people who were dispossessed, or the invading masses who were to be guided and controlled.

If in this achievement there has clearly been a dominant influence, it is that of the Puritans of New England and their descendants. Their livelier faculties have kept the phlegmatic Hollanders from dozing over their pipes; the precocious West owes its substantial vitality to their earnestness of purpose and practical wisdom; and the boastful South has yielded to the force of their principles and their energies.

The true Puritan may be described as " a just man, tenacious of his opinions, whose steadfast mind neither the depraved impulses of disorderly citizens, nor the frown of a threatening tyrant, nor Southern bluster, could shake from its purposes."

You recognize, Mr. President, in this portrait, a translation, nearly literal, of the words of Horace, —

> "Justum et tenacem propositi virum
> Non civium ardor prava jubentium,
> Non vultus instantis tyranni,
> Mente quatit solida: neque Auster."

The lines are almost prophetic; and the words " neque Auster," which appear to have little meaning

60

in their original use, have, in this application, a singular significance.

In the presence of such realities as Plymouth and Massachusetts, how worse than extravagant it seems to dignify the ineffectual operations of an adventurer like Gorges, or the ephemeral and futile visit of a band of outlawed men like the company of Popham, with such appellations as "The source of title to the continent;" "The foundation of the colossal empire of the New World;" "The great event of American history, giving a new direction to the history of the world"!*

A complete list of donors to the library during the last six months is annexed to this Report. There have been received, in the aggregate, three hundred and ninety-one volumes of books, and seventeen hundred and ninety-eight pamphlets; besides some valuable engravings and manuscript documents, and a great number and variety of minor contributions.

---

* These comments on the proceedings at the Popham Celebration were already in type before the writer had seen the "Address of Mr. E. C. Benedict to the New-York Historical Society, Nov. 17, 1863." In that excellent paper, full justice is accorded to the Puritans of New England, and *no less* to the remarkable assumptions contained in the two productions of the Maine orator.

Summary of Donors and Donations.

HON. CHARLES HUDSON, Lexington. — His MS. Reminiscences of Hon. John Davis ; and 4 pamphlets.

WM. H. WHITMORE, Esq., Boston. — His Cavalier Dismounted.

Rev. EDWARD E. HALE, Boston. — An Oil Painting of Dighton Rock, and copy of the Inscription. Also the Boston Daily Advertiser for 1864.

NATHANIEL B. SHURTLEFF, M.D., Boston. — 2 newspapers.

JOSEPH TUCKERMAN, Esq., New York, N.Y. — Lives of Saints, by Alfonso Villegos, 1630.

JOHN H. ELLIS, Esq., Charlestown. — 1 book and 2 pamphlets.

AARON D. HUBBARD, Esq., Boston. — Ridgley's Divinity. 2 volumes, folio.

Rev. RUFUS B. STEBBINS, D.D., Cambridge. — His History of Wilbraham.

Hon. JOHN P. BIGELOW, Boston. — An additional volume of Dictionnaire Universel, &c.

Children of late Rev. J. B. BOOMER, Worcester. — 15 books and 129 pamphlets.

FREDERICK W. PAINE, Esq., Worcester. — 176 books, 49 pamphlets, and various miscellanies.

Professor A. D. BACHE, Washington, D.C. — Report on United-States Coast Survey, for 1862.

HENRY WOODWARD, Esq., Worcester. — 4 books, 7 pamphlets, and 17 portraits of distinguished men.

The STATE OF OHIO. — State documents, 19 volumes ; and 4 pamphlets.

Miss ELIZABETH PARSONS SEVER, Kingston. — An ancient silver watch.

JOEL MUNSELL, Esq., Albany, N.Y. — 5 valuable pamphlets.

A. McF. DAVIS, Esq., New York, N.Y. — The Naval Register of the Rebel States; and rebel newspapers.

Rev. SETH SWEETSER, D.D., Worcester. — 14 pamphlets and 1 broadside.

SAMUEL A. GREEN, M.D., Boston. — 29 pamphlets.

The ROYAL GEOGRAPHICAL SOCIETY, London, G.B. — Journal, vol. xxxiii.; Proceedings, vol. viii., Nos. 3, 4, 5, and 6; and Addresses of the President.

The SOCIETY OF ANTIQUARIES OF LONDON, G.B. — Proceedings. Vol. ii., No. 5.

JAMES PARKER, Esq., Springfield. — The Last Men of the Revolution, with Photographs; also, fac-simile of Connecticut Courant of Oct. 29, 1764.

The LOYAL PUBLICATION SOCIETY, New York, N.Y. — The series of their publications.

Hon. CHARLES SUMNER, Boston. — 1 book, 2 pamphlets, and 1 circular.

The NEW-ENGLAND HISTORIC GENEALOGICAL SOCIETY. — The New-England Historic Genealogical Register. President Lewis's Address, Jan. 4, 1865. Tercentenary Celebration of the Birth of Shakespeare. In Memoriam Edward Everett.

JOHN O. GREEN, M.D., Lowell. — His Memorial of John C. Dalton, M.D.

JOSEPH MASON, Esq., Worcester. — Catalogue of Worcester-County Law Library.

DANIEL TREADWELL, Esq., Cambridge. — His Treatises on the Improvement of Cannon, and the Construction of Hooped Cannon.

Hon. JOHN G. PALFREY, Boston. — His History of New England, vol. iii.

Miss SARAH C. ROCKWOOD, Upton. — 2 books.

Hon. IRA M. BARTON, Worcester. — 1 book, 54 pamphlets, and 3 newspapers.

The MAINE HISTORICAL SOCIETY. — Memorial of Popham Celebration.

CHARLES HADWIN, Worcester. — Book of Discipline of the
Friends, 1785; and 1 pamphlet.
Hon. JOHN D. BALDWIN, Worcester. — Lanman's Dictionary of
Congress; and six valuable publications of Congress.
BENJAMIN BUTMAN, Esq., Worcester. — 12 pamphlets.
Rev. PRESERVED SMITH, Deerfield. — His Sermon delivered at
Warwich, Oct. 12, 1864.
The AMERICAN ACADEMY OF ARTS AND SCIENCES. — Proceed-
ings, from Jan. 28, 1863, to June 14, 1864.
CHARLES A. CHASE, Esq., Worcester. — The Boatswain's Whis-
tle, published at the Sailors' Fair, in Boston; and 3 pamph-
lets.
CHARLES R. LOWELL, Esq., Cambridge. — Dr. Putnam's Address
at the Funeral of Brigadier-General Charles R. Lowell.
Rev. CHARLES BROOKS, Medford. — His History of the Intro-
duction of State Normal Schools in America, and a Prospec-
tive System of National Education for the United States.
The CANADIAN INSTITUTE. — Their Monthly Journal.
The ESSEX INSTITUTE. — Proceedings, vols. iii. and iv., Nos. 3
and 4. Collections, vol. vi., No. 4.
PROVIDENCE ATHENÆUM. — Report of 1864.
Hon. GEORGE W. RICHARDSON, Worcester. — 10 pamphlets and
1 circular.
The SMITHSONIAN INSTITUTION. — New-York Shipping and Com-
mercial List, June to December, 1864.
Mrs. HENRY P. STURGIS, Boston. — 2 books, 37 pamphlets, 29
ballads, and a variety of miscellanies.
Major L. A. LATOUR, Montreal, Canada. — Annuaire de Ville
Marie, 1863.
Rev. EDWIN M. STONE, Providence, R.I. — Rhode Island in the
Rebellion; his Annual Report of the Ministry at Large in
Providence; and 9 Providence City Documents.
HENRY S. THACHER, Northfield. — Book of Dances of the Last
Century.
STATE OF CONNECTICUT. — State Documents, 4 books, 4 pamph-
lets.

MANTON MARBLE, Esq., New York, N.Y. — Handbook of the Democracy, for 1863–64.

The NEW-JERSEY HISTORICAL SOCIETY. — Collections, vol. vi. Proceedings, vol. x., No. 1.

The MASSACHUSETTS HISTORICAL SOCIETY. — Collections, vol. vii., 4th series. Proceedings, 1863–64.

Hon. LEVI LINCOLN, Worcester. — 102 pamphlets; the National Intelligencer for 1864; the Boatswain's Whistle; and Specimens of Electoral Votes of Massachusetts.

EDMUND M. BARTON, Esq., Worcester. — Law Papers taken from Sussex Court House, Va., and a pair of rebel stirrups.

The CHICAGO HISTORICAL SOCIETY. — 10 pamphlets, 1 newspaper, and 7 circulars.

Hon. STEPHEN SALISBURY, Worcester. — Files of the National Intelligencer, Freedman's Advocate, Christian Register, and Gallaudet Guide.

STEPHEN SALISBURY, Jun., Worcester. — 80 magazines and 46 Illustrated London News.

GEORGE LIVERMORE, Esq. — 25 pamphlets.

Miss MARY C. GAY, Suffield, Conn. — Connecticut Courant for 1864, and fac-simile of ditto for Oct. 29, 1764.

OFFICE OF WORCESTER SPY. — A Collection of Sandwich-Island newspapers.

Professor JAMES D. BUTLER, Madison, Wis. — Photographs of an Ancient Medal found in Buffalo County, Wis., with an Historical and Descriptive Account of the same.

JOHN APPLETON, M.D., Boston. — His Journal de Castorland.

The BOSTON ATHENÆUM. — Catalogue of Additions to, during 1863.

JOHN A. McALLISTER, Esq., Philadelphia, Pa. — 2 Photographs of Historical Buildings in Philadelphia.

Mr. E. TUCKER, Worcester. — 1 pamphlet.

HENRY B. DAWSON, Esq., Morrisiana, N.Y. — His Current Fictions Tested by Uncurrent Facts.

The CHARLESTOWN PUBLIC LIBRARY. — Report of the Trustees.

Hon. BENJ. F. THOMAS, Boston. — His Argument for Defence in the Case of United States vs. Franklin W. Smith.

C. T. SAVAGE, Esq., Harvard. — Office Memorandum-book of Samuel P. Savage, 1758, 1759.

The STATE OF MASSACHUSETTS. — State Documents of 1863. Acts and Resolves, 1864.

Rev. ALONZO HILL, D.D., Worcester. — MSS. of Rev. Stephen Bemis, of Harvard; and 1 pamphlet.

HARVARD UNIVERSITY. — Annual Reports of the President and Treasurer.

The BOSTON PUBLIC LIBRARY. — Twelfth Annual Report of the Trustees.

EDWARD JARVIS, M.D., Dorchester. — 11 pamphlets; newspapers and miscellanies.

Rev. CALEB D. BRADLEE, Roxbury. — 10 pamphlets; newspapers, &c.

Hon. ISAAC DAVIS, Worcester. — 100 books and 1,000 pamphlets.

JOHN MELLISH, Esq., Auburn. — The Masonic Mirror, vol. i.

The SECRETARY OF THE NAVY, U.S. — 7 Colored Prints of the Monitors, &c.

GEORGE CHANDLER, M.D., Worcester. — Rebel newspapers; 3 engraved views of Millbury, Mass.; and 3 pamphlets.

The MASSACHUSETTS HORTICULTURAL SOCIETY, by EBEN WRIGHT, Esq., Corresponding Secretary. — Transactions of 1864.

ACADEMY OF NATURAL SCIENCES, Philadelphia. — Proceedings for November and December, 1864.

Miss SOPHIA F. BROWN, Dighton. — Fac-simile of a Drawing of Dighton Rock, made by Joseph Gooding in 1790.

The STATE OF RHODE ISLAND. — 11th Registration Report, 1863.

JAMES H. SALISBURY, M.D., Cleveland, Ohio. — Surgeon-General's Report of Ohio, 1864.

WM. O. SWETT, Esq., Worcester. — The Boston Repertory, for 1805-6.

PLINY E. CHASE, Esq., Philadelphia, Pa. — A MS. Paper on the Unitary Origin of Language.

HENRY PHELPS, Esq., Worcester. — 12 ancient Engravings.

Hon. EMORY WASHBURN, Cambridge. — 2 pamphlets.

Hon. F. W. Lincoln, Jun., Boston. — 10 volumes of Boston City Documents.

Professor Edward Tuckerman, Amherst. — Gazette of United States, 1791–92; Federal Orrery, 1794–96; the Argus, Boston, 1791–93.

R. W. Hooper, Esq., Boston. — Memoir of Hon. William Sturgis.

Mrs. M. Amelia Stone, Cleveland, Ohio. — Her Memoir of Brigadier-General George B. Boomer.

Joseph Sargent, M.D., Worcester. — Le Constitutionnel (newspaper), 1848.

The Mercantile Library Company of Philadelphia. — Forty-second Annual Report.

The Pennsylvania Hospital for the Insane. — Report for 1864.

Wm. F. Poole, Esq., Boston. — 2 Reports of Massachusetts Rifle Club.

Major S. V. Shipman, Madison, Wis. — 3 pamphlets on Military Subjects.

Clement Hugh Hill, Esq., Boston. — 43 pamphlets.

Nathaniel Paine, Esq., Worcester. — Lowth's Lectures on the Sacred Poetry of the Hebrews. 2 volumes, 1787. A collection of Bank Circulars, &c.

American Philosophical Society. — Proceedings, vol. ix., No. 72; and List of Members.

Hon. William Willis, Portland, Me. — His History of Portland; and the new edition of Collections of the Maine Historical Society, vol. i.

Commodore George S. Blake, U.S.N., Newport, R.I. — MS. Essay on the Dighton Rock, by Rev. Charles R. Hale.

D. P. Corey, Esq., Malden. — 25 pamphlets.

Samuel Smith, Esq., Worcester. — 1 rebel paper.

Hon. Robert C. Winthrop, Boston. — 3 pamphlets and a collection of Notices, &c.

Trustees of the Free Public Library of New Bedford. — Thirteenth Annual Report; and Old Dartmouth Centennial Celebration of 1864.

Epes Sargent, Esq., Roxbury. — Reprints of Maps constructed by Martin Behaim and John Schöner in 1492 and 1520.

Professor Laurent Etienne Borring, Copenhagen, Denmark. — His Notices of the Life and Writings of Carl Christian Rafn.

Wm. A. Whitehead, Esq., New York, N.Y. — Hon. R. S. Field's Eulogy on Judge Hornblower.

Samuel L. Taylor, Esq., Philadelphia, Pa. — Report as Librarian of the Historical Society of Pensylvania, for 1864.

George Wales, Esq., Boston. — Catalogue of the Astor Library. 4 volumes.

Hon. Ebenezer Torrey, Fitchburg. — American Magazine and Monthly Chronicle. Philadelphia, 1758 ; a rare volume. Duncan's Cicero ; and 3 pamphlets.

Ebenezer Alden, M.D., Randolph. — The Works of President Jesse Appleton, D.D. 2 volumes in one.

Brigadier-General Charles Devens, Worcester. — A package of Rebel Bonds and Currency, from Richmond.

General Robert Patterson, Philadelphia, Pa. — His Narrative of Campaign in the Valley of the Shenandoah, in 1861.

Wm. R. Deane, Esq., Boston. — His Memoir of Elkanah Watson.

E. French, Esq., New York, N.Y. — 2 pamphlets.

Don Jose F. Ramirez, Mexico. — Geografia de las Lenguas y Carta Etnografica de Mexico.

The Rhode-Island Society for the Encouragement of Domestic Industry. — Transactions of 1864.

John Boyden, Esq., Worcester. — A Political Caricature.

Franklin B. Hough, M.D., Albany, N.Y. — Instructions for taking the Census of New York.

The Proprietors of the Worcester Weekly Spy, Boston Semi-weekly Advertiser, and Fitchburg Sentinel (their papers as issued).

The American Unitarian Association. — Their Monthly Journal.

The United-States Sanitary Commission. — Their Bulletins, &c.

www.ingramcontent.com/pod-product-compliance
Lightning Source LLC
Chambersburg PA
CBHW022021080426
42733CB00007B/674